This Coloring book of mandalas belongs to:

EXPRESS YOUR EMOTIONAL EXPECTATIONS AND WHAT YOU WOULD LIKE TO FEEL AS YOU JOURNEY ALONG THIS PATH.

AFTER EACH EXPERIENCE, YOU CAN WRITE ON THE PAPER YOUR FEELINGS AND EMOTIONS THAT BLOSSOMED WITH THIS MANDALA.

Whispers of the Cosmos

SHARE YOUR FEELINGS:

Enchanting Echoes

SHARE YOUR FEELINGS:

Celestial Harmony

SHARE YOUR FEELINGS:

Dance of Radiance

SHARE YOUR FEELINGS:

Eternal Serenity

SHARE YOUR FEELINGS:

Vibrant Whirlpool

SHARE YOUR FEELINGS:

Infinite Dreamscape

SHARE YOUR FEELINGS:

Spectral Embrace

SHARE YOUR FEELINGS:

Mystical Cascade

SHARE YOUR FEELINGS:

Galactic Embrace

SHARE YOUR FEELINGS:

Stellar Reverie: A Dance of Feelings

SHARE YOUR FEELINGS:

Celestial Symphony: Harmonizing with Emotions

SHARE YOUR FEELINGS:

Nebula Whispers: Unveiling the Emotional Cosmos

SHARE YOUR FEELINGS:

PEN DOWN YOUR FINAL CONCLUSION AND EVERYTHING YOU HAVE FELT ON THIS JOURNEY. IF YOU FEEL UP TO IT, GO AHEAD AND SHARE IT WITH US!